United States Government Accountability Office

Report to the Chairman, Committee on Commerce, Science, and Transportation, U.S. Senate

I0455263

August 2013

POSITIVE TRAIN CONTROL

Additional Authorities Could Benefit Implementation

GAO-13-720

POSITIVE TRAIN CONTROL

Additional Authorities Could Benefit Implementation

GAO Highlights

Highlights of GAO-13-720, a report to the Chairman, Committee on Commerce, Science, and Transportation, U. S. Senate

Why GAO Did This Study

In the wake of a 2008 commuter train collision that resulted in 25 fatalities, RSIA was enacted. It requires major freight railroads, Amtrak, and commuter railroads to install PTC on many major routes by the end of 2015. PTC implementation, overseen by FRA, is a complex endeavor that touches almost every aspect of train operations on major lines. According to FRA, 37 railroads are required to implement PTC. GAO was asked to examine the status of PTC implementation. This report discusses, among other things, railroads' implementation of PTC to date and the challenges, if any, to meeting the 2015 deadline. GAO interviewed representatives from Amtrak, the four largest freight railroads, and seven commuter railroads, selected to represent a mix of locations, ridership levels, and PTC implementation status. GAO also interviewed PTC experts and suppliers, and reviewed FRA's PTC regulatory impact analyses.

What GAO Recommends

Given the implementation challenges railroads face in meeting the deadline, and to help FRA manage its limited resources, Congress should consider amending RSIA as FRA has requested. Specifically, Congress should consider granting FRA the authority to extend the deadline on certain rail lines on a case-by-case basis, grant provisional certification of PTC systems, and approve the use of alternative safety technologies in lieu of PTC to improve safety. DOT reviewed a draft of this report and provided technical comments, which were incorporated as appropriate.

View GAO-13-720. For more information, contact Susan Fleming at (202) 512-2834 or flemings@gao.gov.

What GAO Found

To install positive train control (PTC)—a communications-based system designed to prevent certain types of train accidents caused by human factors—almost all railroads are overlaying their existing infrastructure with PTC components; nonetheless, most railroads report they will miss the December 31, 2015, implementation deadline. Both the Association of American Railroads (AAR) and the Federal Railroad Administration (FRA) have reported that most railroads will not have PTC fully implemented by the deadline. Of the four major freight railroads included in GAO's review, only one expects to meet the 2015 deadline. The other three freight railroads report that they expect to have PTC implemented by 2017 or later. Commuter railroads generally must wait until freight railroads and Amtrak equip the rail lines they operate on, and most of the seven commuter railroads included in this review reported that they do not expect to meet the 2015 deadline. To implement PTC systems that meet the requirements of the Rail Safety Improvement Act of 2008 (RSIA), railroads are developing more than 20 major components that are currently in various stages of development, integrating them, and installing them across the rail network. AAR recently reported that by the end of 2012, railroads had spent $2.8 billion on PTC implementation. To implement PTC, AAR estimates that freight railroads will spend approximately $8 billion in total while the American Public Transportation Association (APTA) estimates that commuter railroads will spend a minimum of $2 billion. Much of the work to implement PTC remains to be done. For example, AAR reported that as of the end of 2012, about a third of wayside interface units, which are needed to communicate data, had been installed and that less than 1 percent of locomotives needing upgrades had been fully equipped.

Most railroads report they will not complete PTC implementation by the 2015 deadline due to a number of complex and interrelated challenges. Many PTC components continue to be in various stages of development, and in order to ensure successful integration of these components, railroads must conduct multiple phases of testing before components are installed across the network. Also, some railroads raised concerns regarding FRA's limited staff resources in two areas: verification of field tests and timely certification of PTC systems. Commuter railroads face additional challenges such as obtaining radio frequency spectrum, which is essential for PTC communications. By attempting to implement PTC by the 2015 deadline while key components are still in development, railroads could be introducing financial and operational risks. For example, officials from railroads and FRA said that without adequate testing, PTC systems might be more prone to reliability issues. To mitigate risks, provide flexibility in meeting the PTC deadline, and better manage limited resources, FRA has requested that Congress amend RSIA to provide additional authorities in implementing PTC. Specifically, FRA requested authority to extend the deadline on certain rail lines, grant provisional certification of PTC systems, and approve the use of alternative safety technologies in lieu of PTC. Flexibility in extending the deadline for certain railroads acknowledges differences in railroads' implementation schedules and may also help FRA better manage its limited resources by, for example, preventing a potential review backlog resulting from most of the railroads' submitting final safety plans at the same time—a concern raised by both freight railroads and FRA.

_____ United States Government Accountability Office

Contents

Abbreviations

AAR	Association of American Railroads
ACSES	Advanced Civil Speed Enforcement System
APTA	American Public Transportation Association
FCC	Federal Communications Commission
FRA	Federal Railroad Administration
GIS	geographical information systems
GPS	Global Positioning System
I-ETMS	Interoperable Electronic Train Management System
NPRM	Notice of Proposed Rulemaking
OMB	Office of Management and Budget
PTC	positive train control
RSIA	Rail Safety Improvement Act of 2008

GAO

U.S. GOVERNMENT ACCOUNTABILITY OFFICE

441 G St. N.W.
Washington, DC 20548

August 16, 2013

The Honorable John D. Rockefeller
Chairman
Committee on Commerce, Science, and Transportation
United States Senate

Dear Mr. Chairman:

In September 2008, a commuter train collided with a freight train in the Chatsworth neighborhood of Los Angeles, California, resulting in 25 deaths and over 100 injuries. In the wake of this accident, which was caused by the operator missing a red signal, the Rail Safety Improvement Act of 2008 (RSIA) was enacted.[1] RSIA mandated the implementation of positive train control (PTC) systems by December 31, 2015, on "mainlines" used to transport inter-city rail passengers, commuters, or any amount of certain toxic materials.[2] PTC is a communications-based system designed to prevent certain types of rail accidents caused by human factors, including train-to-train collisions; trains entering established work zones, which could cause roadway worker casualties or equipment damage; and derailments caused by exceeding safe speeds. PTC technology can automatically slow or stop a train that is not being operated safely due to some types of operator errors or a switch left in the wrong position.

PTC system implementation is a complex and costly endeavor that touches almost every part of major rail lines and almost every aspect of their train operations. Railroad representatives and experts have reported that PTC implementation is the biggest change in the railroad industry since it transitioned from steam to diesel locomotives in the mid-20th century. According to FRA, railroads required to implement PTC must do so on over 60,000 of approximately 160,000 miles of track nationwide. In addition, FRA has reported that railroads must design, produce, and install more than 20 major PTC components, such as data radios for

---

[1]Pub. L. No. 110-432, div. A, 122 Stat. 4848.

[2]RSIA defines mainlines as those carrying 5 million or more gross tons of freight annually and grants FRA the authority to provide additional criteria for passenger routes. Toxic materials are referred to as either toxic-by-inhalation or poison-by-inhalation materials.

GAO-13-720 Positive Train Control

locomotive communication, locomotive management computers, and back office servers as part of the PTC implementation.

We, along with the Federal Railroad Administration (FRA), have noted the challenges railroads face in implementing PTC by the 2015 deadline. In December 2010, we reported that much work remained for railroads to meet the 2015 implementation deadline.[3] Likewise, in August 2012, FRA issued a report to Congress and concluded that, due to many obstacles, the majority of railroads will be unable to meet the deadline.[4] Congress has considered, but has not passed, extensions to this deadline.[5]

FRA provides regulatory oversight of U.S. railroad safety and is responsible for overseeing PTC implementation. As part of its implementation of RSIA, FRA conducted three rulemakings and analyzed the economic impact of two final rules. FRA's economic analyses of these rules calculated the costs of PTC implementation and discussed various benefits that railroads may attain by implementing PTC. Such benefits could include avoided property damage levels due to the avoidance of accidents and operational efficiencies from PTC that could result in cost savings to the railroad, known in the industry as "business benefits."[6] Railroad industry representatives testified before Congress that PTC will not result in business benefits and that business benefits can be achieved through other means, such as technologies independent of PTC.[7]

To better understand the impact of RSIA and FRA's associated rulemakings on railroads, you asked us to examine the status of PTC

---

[3]GAO, *Rail Safety: Federal Railroad Administration Should Report on Risks to the Successful Implementation of Mandated Safety Technology*, GAO-11-133 (Washington, D.C.: Dec. 15, 2010).

[4]FRA, *Report to Congress, Positive Train Control Implementation Status, Issues, and Impacts* (August 2012).

[5]In the 112th Congress, bills to delay the deadline were considered in both houses of Congress, but were not enacted. See, H.R. 7, 112th Cong. (2012); S. 1813, 112th Cong. (2011). In the current Congress, a Senate bill was introduced to extend the deadline until December 31, 2020. See S. 1462, 113th Cong. (2013).

[6]From this point on in this report, we refer to these operational efficiencies and cost savings as "business benefits."

[7]Joint Statement of the Association of American Railroads and Norfolk Southern Railway before the U.S. House of Representatives Committee on Transportation and Infrastructure, March 17, 2011.

implementation and the costs and benefits of the PTC rule, including business benefits. This report discusses (1) how railroads are implementing PTC and the challenges, if any, to meeting the 2015 implementation deadline, and (2) FRA's estimates of the benefits and costs of PTC and the extent to which railroads might be able to leverage PTC technology to achieve business benefits.

To examine how railroads are implementing PTC, and any challenges they are facing, we reviewed documents and interviewed officials from FRA and representatives from railroad associations including the Association of American Railroads and American Public Transportation Association. We interviewed representatives from the four largest freight railroads—BNSF Railway, CSX Corporation, Union Pacific, and Norfolk Southern. We interviewed representatives from seven commuter railroads, which we selected to represent a range of geographic locations, levels of ridership, PTC implementation status, and operations, including those operating on tracks owned by all four of the largest Class I railroads and the National Passenger Railroad Corporation (Amtrak). We also interviewed Amtrak representatives. We interviewed or received written responses to our interview questions from PTC suppliers and independent PTC experts that we selected based on involvement with PTC and recommendations from FRA, associations, and others.

To determine how FRA estimated the benefits and costs of PTC, we interviewed FRA officials and experts, among others, and evaluated proposed and final regulatory impact analyses for the 2010 and 2012 PTC rules. We reviewed the regulatory analyses supporting the rules using standard economic principles and Office of Management and Budget (OMB) economic guidance (*Circular A-4*) as criteria. See appendix I for more detailed information about our scope and methodology.

We conducted this performance audit from October 2012 to August 2013 in accordance with generally accepted government auditing standards. Those standards require that we plan and perform the audit to obtain sufficient, appropriate evidence to provide a reasonable basis for our findings and conclusions based on our audit objectives. We believe that the evidence obtained provides a reasonable basis for our findings and conclusions based on our audit objectives.

Background

Railroads and Supporting Infrastructure

The U.S. railroad industry consists mostly of freight railroads but also serves passengers. Freight railroads are divided into classes based on revenue.[8] Class I freight railroads earn the most revenue and generally provide long-haul freight service.[9] Freight railroads operate over approximately 160,000 miles of track and own most of the track in the United States; a notable exception is the Northeast Corridor, between Washington, D.C., and Boston, Massachusetts, which Amtrak predominantly owns. Amtrak provides intercity passenger rail service in 46 states and the District of Columbia and operates on 21,000 miles of track. Commuter railroads serve passengers traveling within large metropolitan areas and most operate over track infrastructure owned by Amtrak or freight railroads for at least some portion of their operations. Specifically, 9 commuter railroads operate over Amtrak-owned infrastructure. Sixteen commuter railroads operate over infrastructure owned by freight railroads.[10,11]

U.S. freight and passenger trains often share track, dispatchers, and signals that control train movement. Some railroads also use additional technologies to improve efficiency and achieve business benefits. Currently, dispatchers in centralized offices issue train movement authorities that allow trains to enter specific track segments, or blocks. These authorities are communicated to train operators through signals alongside the track, or in non-signaled territory through track warrants generally issued by verbal radio communication (see fig. 1). Railroads also use additional technologies to maximize operational efficiencies. These include:

---

[8]Currently, there are seven Class I railroads operating in the United States. There are also over 500 smaller freight railroads in the United States, called short line and regional railroads, which earn less revenue and generally haul freight shorter distances. While we met with the American Short Line and Regional Railroad Association, we did not meet with individual short line or regional railroads. Short line and regional railroads that run on tracks equipped with PTC and travel over 20 miles are required to install PTC by 2020. 49 C.F.R. § 236.1006(b)(4).

[9]From this point on, we refer to Class I railroads as "freight railroads."

[10]GAO, *Commuter Rail: Many Factors Influence Liability and Indemnity Provisions, and Options Exist to Facilitate Negotiations.* GAO-09-282 (Washington, D.C.: Feb. 24, 2009).

[11]There are currently a total of 28 commuter railroads.

GAO-13-720 Positive Train Control

- *Computer-assisted dispatching* so dispatchers can, among other things, optimally synchronize schedules, allowing trains on single track to "meet and pass" one another safely and efficiently, thereby minimizing delays and improving on-time performance.

- *Energy management systems* that analyze train location and track grade and curvature information to calculate the train's most fuel-efficient speed throughout the trip.

These technologies can lead to business benefits for the railroad as well as benefits for society at large. As we have reported in the past, diversion of freight traffic from highways to rail potentially increases highway safety and reduces highway congestion and energy consumption.[12]

---

[12]GAO, *Intercity Passenger and Freight Rail: Better Data and Communication of Uncertainties Can Help Decision Makers Understand Benefits and Trade-offs of Programs and Policies,* GAO-11-290 (Washington, D.C.: Feb. 24, 2011).

Figure 1: Key Components of Current U.S. Railroad Operations

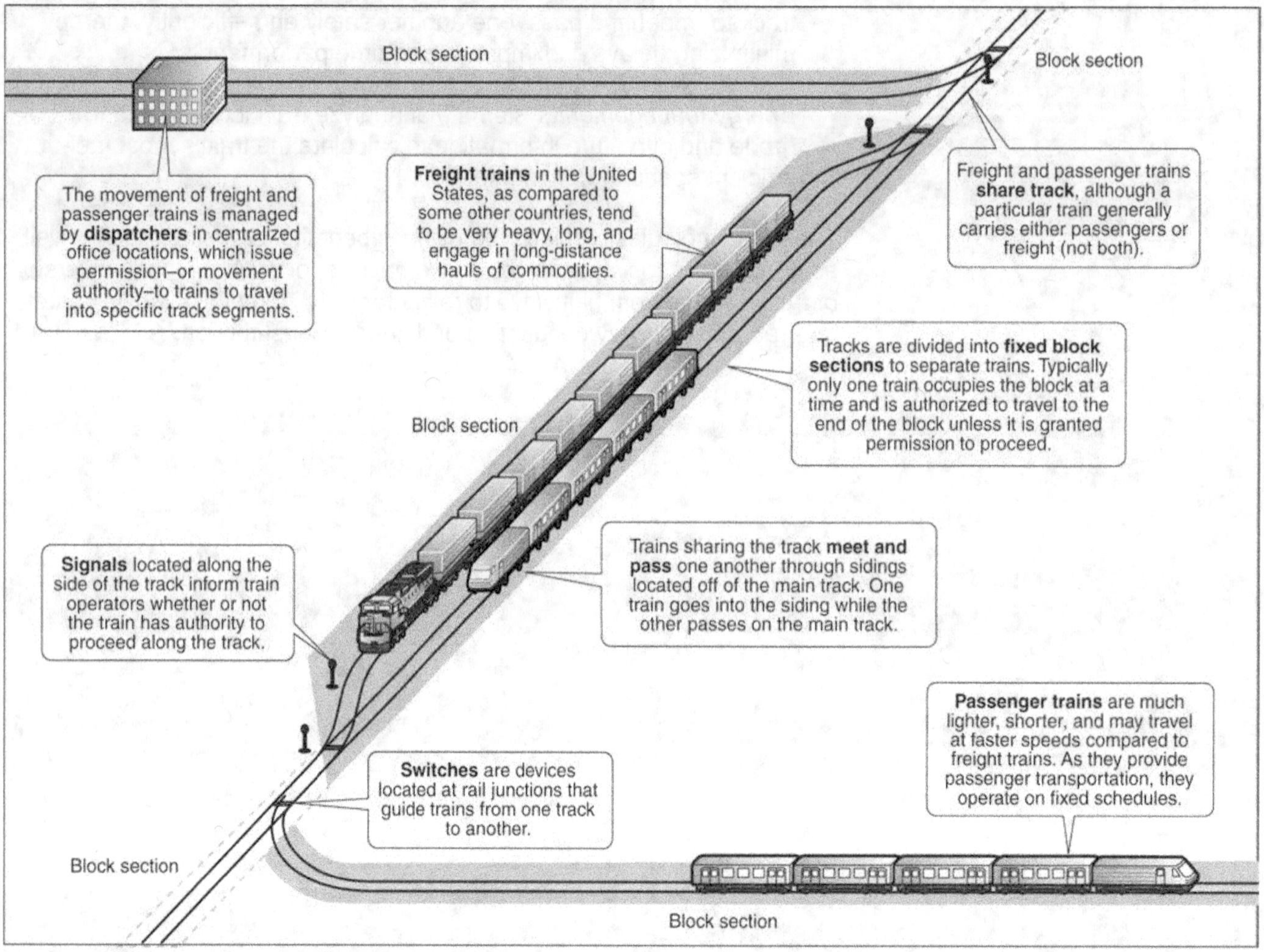

The movement of freight and passenger trains is managed by **dispatchers** in centralized office locations, which issue permission–or movement authority–to trains to travel into specific track segments.

Freight trains in the United States, as compared to some other countries, tend to be very heavy, long, and engage in long-distance hauls of commodities.

Freight and passenger trains **share track**, although a particular train generally carries either passengers or freight (not both).

Tracks are divided into **fixed block sections** to separate trains. Typically only one train occupies the block at a time and is authorized to travel to the end of the block unless it is granted permission to proceed.

Signals located along the side of the track inform train operators whether or not the train has authority to proceed along the track.

Trains sharing the track **meet and pass** one another through sidings located off of the main track. One train goes into the siding while the other passes on the main track.

Switches are devices located at rail junctions that guide trains from one track to another.

Passenger trains are much lighter, shorter, and may travel at faster speeds compared to freight trains. As they provide passenger transportation, they operate on fixed schedules.

Block section

Block section

Block section

Block section

Source: GAO.

Rail Safety

Although train accidents have generally been on the decline in recent years, human factors such as train operators missing a red signal or exceeding allowable speeds, or train crews leaving a switch in the wrong position can lead to significant damage and loss of life.[13] Overall, rail safety—measured by the train accident rate per million train miles—has improved markedly since 1980.[14] According to FRA data, 2012 was the safest year in railroad history. Even with the significant reduction in accident rates, on average almost 300 people were reported injured and about 10 people were reported killed in train accidents each year, from 2003 through 2012.[15]

PTC is a computer-based technology that uses a communications system to monitor and control train movements to minimize human factor errors. Prior to the enactment of the RSIA in 2008, railroads developed and tested several PTC systems but deployed them on a limited basis.[16] For example, in 1998, while Amtrak was upgrading the Northeast Corridor to enable operation of high-speed passenger trains—a service known today as Acela—FRA directed Amtrak to install a new train control system on some portions of the corridor as a safety measure. Amtrak worked with suppliers to develop a form of PTC—known as Advanced Civil Speed Enforcement System (ACSES)—and deployed this system on the Northeast Corridor.

Railway Safety Improvement Act of 2008

In wake of the Chatsworth rail accident in September 2008 and other high-profile rail accidents, RSIA was enacted. RSIA, among other things, required railroads to install PTC by December 31, 2015, on mainlines used to transport inter-city rail passengers, commuters, or any amount of

---

[13]In January 2005, a train accident in Graniteville South Carolina caused by a train crew leaving a switch in the wrong position resulted in 9 deaths and 554 people being taken to local hospitals. According to the National Transportation Safety Board, the total damages resulting from the accident were over $6.9 million.

[14]See GAO Rail Safety: Preliminary Observations on Federal Rail Safety Oversight and Implementation of Positive Train Control. GAO-13-679T (Washington, D.C.: June 19, 2013).

[15]These figures do not include highway-railroad grade crossings or trespasser accidents.

[16]BNSF's predecessor, Burlington Northern, deployed Advanced Railroad Electronic System (ARES) on 250 miles of track in northern Minnesota and was operational from 1987 to 1993. Although ARES tested successfully it was never deployed on a wide scale due to cost and lack of technical maturity. In 1994 BNSF and Union Pacific worked together to develop a system called Positive Train Separation. Again the cost and technical maturity prevented deployment. BNSF began development of another PTC system—Electronic Train Management System (ETMS)—in 2003 and FRA conditionally approved this system in 2006.

toxic-by-inhalation materials.[17] RSIA requires railroads to install PTC systems, which are designed to prevent train-to-train collisions and derailments caused by exceeding safe speeds. PTC must also be designed to protect rail workers by preventing trains from entering work zones as well as to prevent the movement of trains through switches left in the wrong position. PTC's communications-based system links various components, namely locomotive computers, wayside units along the side of the track, and dispatch systems in centralized office locations (see fig. 2). Through these components, PTC is able to communicate a train's location, speed restrictions, and movement authorities, and can slow or stop a train that is not being operated safely. For example, a PTC system could have prevented the 2008 Chatsworth accident by first alerting the operator that the train was approaching a red signal and then stopping the train before passing the red signal. However, it should be noted that there are types of accidents, such as highway-railroad crossing accidents and trespasser deaths, that PTC technology is not designed to prevent. According to FRA, highway-railroad crossing and trespasser deaths account for 95 percent of all rail-related fatalities.

---

[17]Toxic-by-inhalation materials are gases or liquids such as chlorine and anhydrous ammonia that are especially hazardous if released into the atmosphere.

Figure 2: Basic Operation of a Positive Train Control (PTC) System

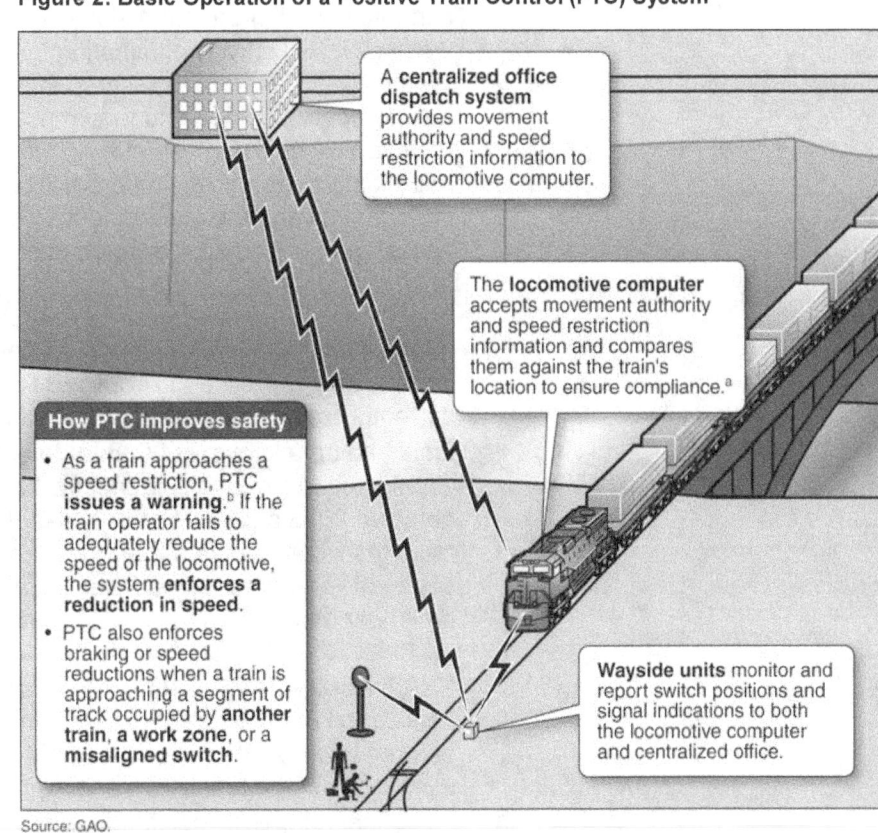

A **centralized office dispatch system** provides movement authority and speed restriction information to the locomotive computer.

The **locomotive computer** accepts movement authority and speed restriction information and compares them against the train's location to ensure compliance.[a]

How PTC improves safety

- As a train approaches a speed restriction, PTC **issues a warning**.[b] If the train operator fails to adequately reduce the speed of the locomotive, the system **enforces a reduction in speed**.
- PTC also enforces braking or speed reductions when a train is approaching a segment of track occupied by **another train**, a **work zone**, or a **misaligned switch**.

Wayside units monitor and report switch positions and signal indications to both the locomotive computer and centralized office.

Source: GAO.

[a]Train location information is determined through various methods depending on the specific PTC system, including through satellite-based positioning systems and sensors installed along the track.

[b]Although the law does not require PTC systems to issue such warnings, the PTC systems that most railroads are implementing will do so.

RSIA does not require railroads to implement the same PTC system; however, the various PTC systems must meet the PTC system functionality requirements.[18] There are two primary ways PTC can be implemented—as an overlay or as a standalone system. An overlay system involves installing PTC over existing track equipment to work in conjunction with the existing signal system and the train's current method

---

[18]Under RSIA, PTC must be designed to prevent train-to-train collisions, over-speed derailments, incursions into work zone limits, and the movement of a train through a switch left in the wrong position.

of operations. A standalone system involves taking information currently communicated through the signal system and putting it onboard the locomotive, effectively eliminating the need for the existing signal system. Whatever PTC system a railroad implements, RSIA requires that systems be interoperable, meaning they must be able to communicate with one another so trains can seamlessly move across track owned by different railroads with potentially different PTC systems. Interoperability is important given that, according to FRA, there are 37 freight, intercity passenger, and commuter railroads that are required to implement PTC.

To implement the requirements of RSIA, FRA has conducted three rulemakings that resulted in: (1) a 2010 final rule, (2) a 2012 final rule, and (3) a 2012 Notice of Proposed Rulemaking (NPRM), which is currently not finalized (see fig. 3).[19] In the original 2010 rule, FRA used facts and data known in 2008 to determine where PTC implementation should occur. Recognizing that traffic levels and routing could change between 2008 and the statutory deadline in 2015, the 2010 rule provided railroads with the option to request an amendment to not equip a track segment where the railroad was initially required to install PTC, but may no longer be required to do so. In order for certain rail segments to be excluded, the segments would need to pass two qualifying tests.[20] After FRA finalized the 2010 rule, the Association of American Railroads (AAR) challenged the two qualifying tests in a lawsuit, and FRA and AAR entered into a settlement agreement in which FRA agreed to propose elimination of the tests.[21] The two qualifying tests were eliminated in the 2012 final rule; as a result, railroads do not have to implement PTC on rail segments that will not transport toxic-by-inhalation materials or passengers as of December 31, 2015. The FRA rulemaking that is

---

[19]75 Fed. Reg. 2598 (Jan. 15, 2010); 77 Fed Reg. 28,285 (May 14, 2012); 77 Fed. Reg. 73589 (Dec. 11, 2012). FRA also published amendments to the 2010 final rule. See 75 Fed. Reg. 59108 (Sept. 27, 2010).

[20]These two qualifying tests were the alternative route analysis test and the residual risk analysis test. Under the alternative route analysis test, a railroad would have had to establish that rerouting toxic materials to one or more alternative track segments was justified. Under the residual risk analysis test, a railroad would have had to show that without a PTC system, the remaining risk on the track segment was less than the national average equivalent risk per route mile on track segments required to be equipped with PTC systems due to statutory reasons other than passenger traffic presence.

[21]AAR is challenging FRA's determination to use 2008 as the base year, arguing that it rests on a fundamental legal error and was arbitrary and capricious. As of our reporting date, the lawsuit is pending.

GAO-13-720 Positive Train Control

currently under way addresses how railroads will handle en-route failures of PTC equipment, among other things.

Figure 3: Positive Train Control's Regulatory Timeline, 2008–2015

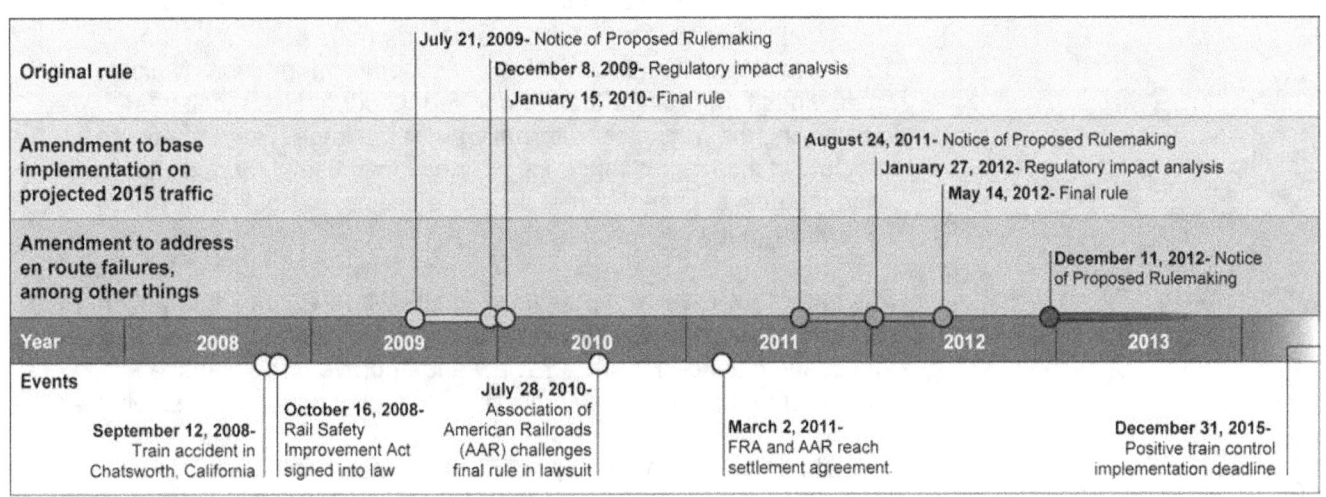

Source: GAO.

In accordance with Executive Order 12866, FRA prepared economic analyses—also known as regulatory impact analyses—to assess the benefits and costs of PTC before promulgating regulations.[22] Specifically, FRA issued two regulatory impact analyses evaluating final rules—one dated December 2009 evaluating the 2010 final rule and one dated January 2012 evaluating the 2012 final rule.[23] Executive orders and OMB guidance direct agencies to assess the benefits and costs of regulatory alternatives. Agencies should generally select the regulatory approach that maximizes net benefits to society, unless a statute requires otherwise. OMB developed guidelines to encourage good regulatory impact analysis and to standardize the way that benefits and costs of federal regulations are measured and reported.[24] OMB guidelines generally direct agencies, in analyzing the impacts of rules, to, among

[22]See Executive Order 12866, 58 Fed. Reg. 51735 (Oct. 4, 1993).

[23]FRA also prepared a regulatory impact analysis for the 2012 Notice of Proposed Rulemaking.

[24]OMB. *Circular A-4* (Sept. 17, 2003).

GAO-13-720 Positive Train Control

other things: measure the potential social benefits and costs of regulatory alternatives incremental to a "baseline," (i.e., the conditions that would exist in the absence of the proposed regulation); analyze a range of alternatives; identify and quantitatively analyze key uncertainties associated with the estimates of benefits and costs; and provide documentation that the analysis is based on the best reasonably obtainable scientific, technical, and economic information available. OMB guidelines further state that a good regulatory analysis includes identifying the regulatory alternative with the largest net benefits to society. It also states that such information is useful for decision makers and the public, even when economic efficiency is not the only or the overriding public policy objective.

As part of overseeing railroads' progress with PTC implementation, FRA is also responsible for reviewing railroads' PTC-related plans. Railroads must submit and FRA must review and approve three plans: a PTC development plan, a PTC implementation plan, and a PTC safety plan.

- The PTC development plan[25] describes, among other things, the PTC system a railroad intends to implement to satisfy the PTC regulatory requirements. According to its August 2012 report, FRA's approval of the development plans took nearly 18 months to complete.

- The PTC implementation plan describes a railroad's plan for installation of its planned PTC system. RSIA required railroads to submit these plans within 18 months (by April 16, 2010), and FRA to review and approve or disapprove them within 90 days.

- The PTC safety plan[26] includes a railroad's plans for testing the system, as well as information about safety hazards and risks the system will address, among other things. By approving a safety plan, FRA certifies a railroad's PTC system, a precondition for operating the PTC system in revenue service. Although FRA set no specific deadline for railroads to submit the safety plans, according to FRA, railroads must submit their safety plans with sufficient time for approval before the December 31, 2015, PTC implementation

---

[25]49 C.F.R. §§ 236.1009, 236.1013.

[26]49 C.F.R. §§ 236.1009, 236.1015.

GAO-13-720 Positive Train Control

deadline. In its August 2012 report, FRA reported to need about 6 to 9 months to review each safety plan.

Almost All Railroads Are Installing PTC Overlay Systems but Face Challenges in Meeting the 2015 Implementation Deadline

Railroads Are Generally Implementing PTC as an Overlay System for Feasibility Reasons

Although there are two primary types of PTC systems—overlay and standalone— that functionally meet the PTC requirements in RSIA, almost all railroads required to install PTC are installing overlay systems. Railroad representatives told us they chose to install PTC as an overlay system because it was more feasible to meet the PTC implementation deadline than a standalone system. An overlay system allows railroads to install PTC components over existing rail infrastructure and operate the train in accordance with the existing signals and operations in the event of a PTC system failure.

Of the various PTC overlay systems that have been developed, all seven major freight railroads in the United States plan to implement Interoperable Electronic Train Management System (I-ETMS), which will account for most of the approximately 60,000 miles.[27] Amtrak is implementing Advanced Civil Speed Enforcement System (ACSES) on the Northeast Corridor.[28] Although ACSES and I-ETMS are functionally similar, they differ technologically. To determine train location, ACSES relies on track-embedded transponders while I-ETMS uses Global Positioning System (GPS) information (see fig. 4). Since most commuter

[27]Four railroads—BNSF Railway, CSX Corporation, Union Pacific, and Norfo k Southern—are together developing the standards for I-ETMS.

[28]Amtrak installed Incremental Train Control System (ITCS), another communication-based overlay PTC System, on its Michigan line.

railroads run over tracks owned by freight railroads or Amtrak, they are largely implementing the same systems developed by the freight railroads or Amtrak. For example, eight commuter rail systems that operate over Amtrak infrastructure on the Northeast Corridor—including major commuter systems in the New York City, Philadelphia, and Boston areas—are installing ACSES.

Figure 4: Basic Operation of the Interoperable Electronic Train Management System (I-ETMS)

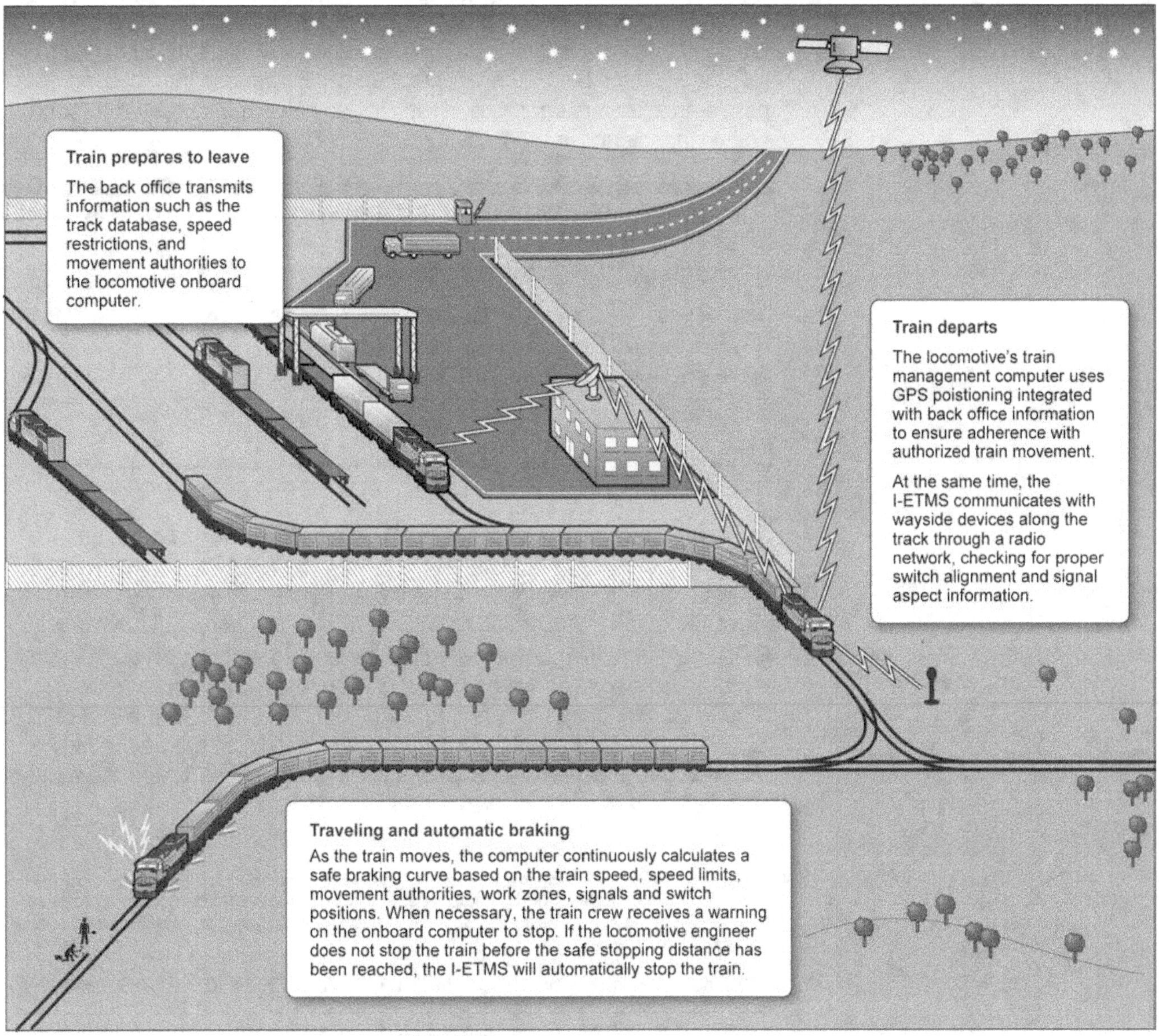

Train prepares to leave

The back office transmits information such as the track database, speed restrictions, and movement authorities to the locomotive onboard computer.

Train departs

The locomotive's train management computer uses GPS poistioning integrated with back office information to ensure adherence with authorized train movement.

At the same time, the I-ETMS communicates with wayside devices along the track through a radio network, checking for proper switch alignment and signal aspect information.

Traveling and automatic braking

As the train moves, the computer continuously calculates a safe braking curve based on the train speed, speed limits, movement authorities, work zones, signals and switch positions. When necessary, the train crew receives a warning on the onboard computer to stop. If the locomotive engineer does not stop the train before the safe stopping distance has been reached, the I-ETMS will automatically stop the train.

Source: GAO.

FRA has reported that in order to implement PTC, railroads must design, produce, and install more than 20 major components such as data radios for locomotive communication, locomotive management computers, and back office servers. Once these components are developed and integrated, PTC must then be installed on rail lines throughout the country, which involves upgrading and installing thousands of items, as well as replacing approximately 12,000 signals (see table 1). Adding to the complexity of PTC installation is the need to ensure that individual railroad systems are fully interoperable, which requires that the potential problems across railroads be identified, isolated, and corrected through testing in labs and in the field.

Table 1: Positive Train Control's Scale of Deployment—Number of Items Requiring Upgrade or Installation

Type of equipment	Total number
Locomotives	18,000
Wayside interface units	38,000
Signal installation /replacement	12,000
Signal modifications	4,900
Back office and dispatch systems	30

Source: FRA.

Railroads have invested billions in PTC implementation to-date, but anticipate spending billions more.[29] In May 2013, AAR reported that by the end of 2012, railroads had spent about $2.8 billion on PTC implementation.[30] According to AAR, the total cost to freight railroads for PTC implementation is estimated to be approximately $8 billion.[31] Despite the billions railroads have invested, much of the work to implement PTC remains to be done. For example, AAR reported that as of the end of 2012, about a third of wayside interface units— which are needed to communicate data—had been installed. In addition, AAR reported that as

---

[29]Freight railroads largely fund capital expenses with their own funds. According to AAR, U.S. freight railroads reinvest over $20 billion each year of their own revenues on their network.

[30]This includes cost information from the Alaska Railroad, BNSF, Canadian National, Canadian Pacific, CSX, Kansas City Southern, Norfolk Southern, and Union Pacific. See Association of American Railroads (AAR), PTC Implementation: The Railroad Industry Cannot Install PTC on the Entire Network by the 2015 Deadline, May 2013 Update.

[31]Testimony of Edward R. Hamberger, President and Chief Executive Officer, Association of American Railroads, before the United States Senate Committee on Commerce, Science, and Transportation, June 19, 2013. We did not independently verify these cost figures.

of the end of 2012, less than 1 percent of locomotives needing upgrades had been fully equipped.[32]

Most Railroads Report They Will Miss the 2015 PTC Implementation Deadline Due to a Number of Challenges

Most railroads report they will not complete PTC implementation by the 2015 deadline due to numerous interrelated challenges caused by the breadth and complexity of PTC. Both AAR and FRA have reported that most railroads will not have PTC fully implemented by the deadline. Of the four major freight railroads we included in our review, BNSF is the only railroad expecting to meet the 2015 deadline.[33] According to BNSF representatives, it is on schedule to meet the 2015 deadline because of its extensive experience working on PTC prior to RSIA, its iterative build and test approach, and the concurrent development of its PTC dispatching and back office systems.[34] Of the three remaining freight railroads we spoke to, representatives believe they will likely have PTC fully implemented by 2017 or later. In addition, while Amtrak officials report that they anticipate full PTC implementation on their Northeast Corridor and Michigan lines by the end of 2015, they noted it is unlikely they will have equipped the approximately 300 locomotives that will run on I-ETMS freight lines by the deadline. Commuter railroads generally must wait to equip their locomotives until freight railroads and Amtrak equip the rail lines that commuter railroads generally operate on. Four of the seven commuter railroads we included in our review reported that they will be unable to meet the 2015 PTC implementation deadline.[35]

Challenges to meeting the 2015 deadline are complex and interrelated. For instance, many of the PTC components had not been developed before RSIA was enacted, and some continue to be in various stages of development. In addition, all components, once developed must be

---

[32]AAR, *PTC Implementation: The Railroad Industry Cannot Install PTC on the Entire Nationwide Network by the 2015 Deadline*, May 2013 Update.

[33]However, BNSF officials note that regulatory considerations such as the outcome of FRA's current rulemaking could affect their ability to meet the deadline.

[34]A BNSF representative explained that they began working on ETMS, a predecessor to I-ETMS, in 2003.

[35]Metrolink officials said they pledged to be the first commuter railroad with a fully operational PTC system and meet the existing FRA PTC requirements after their railroad's 2008 Chatsworth accident and are working closely with FRA, freight railroads, and PTC suppliers to meet the 2015 deadline.

assembled and integrated to achieve the overall safety function of PTC. Likewise, the steps involved with implementing PTC are interrelated, with delays or problems with one component or process resulting in additional delays. Railroad representatives told us that once all the components have been assembled, integrated, and tested for reliability, rolling out and phasing in a PTC system into each railroad's network will take a considerable amount of time. For example, Amtrak first conducted a demonstration test of its PTC system on its Michigan line in 1996, but it was 5 years later, in 2001, when the system was put into service.[36] Finally, FRA's resources and ability to help facilitate implementation by the 2015 PTC deadline are limited. Below is a discussion of these key interrelated challenges.

- *Developing system components and PTC installation.* Some PTC components are still in development, most notably the I-ETMS back office server. One or more of these servers will be installed in over a dozen railroads' back offices and are needed to communicate vital information between the back office, locomotives, and waysides. According to AAR and the railroads, back office system delays are due to system complexity, interfaces to other systems, and lack of supplier resources.[37] Nearly all of the freight railroads included in our review anticipate they will not have a final version of the back office system until 2014 and have identified it as one of the critical factors preventing them from meeting the deadline. In addition to component development, PTC installation is a time- and resource-consuming process. For example, railroads collectively will have to install approximately 38,000 wayside interface units. According to AAR and freight railroads, the volume and complexity of installing these signals is another significant reason most railroads cannot meet the 2015 deadline. Railroads have also encountered unexpected delays while installing PTC. For example, the Federal Communications Commission (FCC) recently requested railroads halt their construction of radio antennae towers to allow FCC to consider how to implement oversight of the towers being installed for PTC. According to FRA and AAR officials, FCC requested that railroads halt construction on

---

[36]This system is called ITCS and is currently in operation between Porter, Indiana, and Kalamazoo, Michigan.

[37]In particular, AAR has reported that railroads rely on a small number of companies with limited capacity, partially due to the small number of professionals with knowledge of both technology and railroad operations.

antennae towers that have not gone through the environmental evaluation process, including tribal notice, while FCC considers ways to streamline the process.[38] FRA officials told us they did not anticipate this issue. AAR and FRA officials report they are working together with FCC to find a solution that meets the goals behind the process while still allowing for timely PTC deployment. However, the impact of halting construction on the towers may result in additional delays in railroads' time frames.

- *System integration and field testing.* Successful PTC implementation will require numerous components to work together, many of which are first-generation technologies being designed and developed for PTC. All components must properly function when integrated or the PTC system could fail. To ensure successful integration, railroads must conduct multiple phases of testing—first in a laboratory environment, then in the field—before installation across the network. Representatives from all of the freight railroads we spoke with expressed concern with the reliability of PTC and emphasized the importance of field testing to ensure that the system performs the way it is intended and that potential defects are identified, corrected, and re-tested. One railroad representative we spoke with said that in some field tests, the PTC system components behaved differently than in the laboratory tests because labs do not reflect field conditions completely. Identifying the source of these types of problems is an iterative process; consequently, correcting the problems and re-testing can be time-consuming and potentially further contribute to railroads not meeting the 2015 deadline.

- *FRA resources.* Although most railroads we spoke with said they have worked closely with FRA throughout the PTC implementation process, some railroads cited concerns with FRA's limited staffing resources. These concerns focused on two of FRA's responsibilities. First, FRA officials must verify field testing of PTC. However, FRA reported that it lacks the staffing resources to embed a dedicated FRA inspector at

---

[38]According to FRA, each PTC tower must go through an FCC approval process, which includes a review of compliance with the National Environmental Policy Act (NEPA) and other laws. For example, depending on the tower's location, the FCC approval process may also include a review to ensure compliance with the National Historic Preservation Act. FCC notifies federally recognized tr bes, Native Hawaiian Organizations, and State Historic Preservation Officers of proposed communications towers and allows these organizations to inform stakeholders about their concerns.

each railroad for regular, detailed, and unfiltered reporting on railroads' PTC progress.[39] To address the lack of staff to verify field-testing, FRA has taken an audit approach to field testing, whereby railroads submit field test results for approval as part of their safety plans and FRA staff select plans to evaluate the accuracy of the results. Second, before a railroad can operate a PTC system in revenue service, it must be FRA certified, and FRA must approve the railroad's final safety plan. FRA set no specific deadline for railroads to submit the safety plans, and according to FRA, to-date only one railroad has submitted a final safety plan, which FRA has approved.[40] As it reported in its 2012 report to Congress, FRA's PTC staff consists of 10 PTC specialists and 1 supervisor who are responsible for the review and approval of all PTC final safety plans.[41] FRA also reported that this work covers the 37 railroads implementing PTC on over 60,000 miles of track. FRA and railroads have expressed concern that railroads will submit their final safety plans to FRA at approximately the same time, resulting in a potential review backlog particularly since each plan is expected to consist of hundreds of pages of detailed technical information. FRA officials told us that they are dedicated to the timely approval of safety plans and that their oversight will not impede railroads from meeting the deadline.[42] However, railroads report that their time frames are based on a quick turnaround in approvals from FRA. If approvals are delayed, it could be a further setback in railroads' PTC implementation.

Generally commuter railroads face these same PTC implementation challenges, as well as others. First, because commuter railroads are using the PTC systems developed by freight railroads and Amtrak, they are captive in many respects to the pace of developments of those entities and have few means to influence implementation schedules. Commuter railroads also face challenges in funding PTC implementation

---

[39]FRA, Report to Congress, Positive Train Control Implementation Status, Issues, and Impacts. August 2012.

[40] Select railroads told us they have submitted draft portions of their safety plans to FRA for preliminary review to expedite the process. This way FRA staff will be familiar with portions of the plan that are common across plans before the finalized plan is submitted.

[41] According to FRA, 3 senior technical staff will also assist with the reviews.

[42]FRA must review safety plans within 180 days of the filing. If FRA is unable to meet this deadline, it must provide a statement of reasons and projected deadline for its review. See 49 C.F.R. § 236.1009(j).

due to the overall lack of federal funding available to make investments in commuter rail and limited sources of revenue. Most commuter railroads are non-profit, public operations that are funded by passenger fares and contributions from federal, state, and local sources. Economic challenges such as the recession have eroded state and local revenue sources that traditionally supported capital expenses. In addition, according the American Public Transportation Association (APTA), commuter railroads face competing expenses such as state of good repair upgrades, leaving them with limited funding to implement PTC. According to APTA, collectively, PTC implementation will cost commuter railroads a minimum of $2 billion. Finally, commuter railroads report that obtaining radio frequency spectrum—essential for PTC communications—can be a lengthy and difficult process.[43] FCC directed commuter railroads to secure spectrum on the secondary market.[44] According to the FCC, spectrum is available in the secondary market to meet PTC needs.[45] While freight railroads have secured most of the spectrum needed for PTC implementation, commuter railroads have reported difficulty acquiring spectrum in the 220 megahertz (MHz) band, which is required to operate the data radios that communicate information between PTC components.[46] In particular, railroad representatives said that obtaining spectrum is a critical challenge in high-density urban areas. Without acquiring sufficient spectrum, railroads may be unable to adequately test

---

[43]Radio frequency spectrum is the medium for wireless communications and supports a vast array of commercial and governmental services. Commercial entities use spectrum to provide a variety of wireless services, including mobile voice and data, paging, broadcast television and radio, and satellite services.

[44]Secondary Market policies and rules allow spectrum permit licensees to share their spectrum resource through spectrum lease arrangements. Users negotiate their own terms for sharing spectrum and FCC tracks these secondary market transactions. *Spectrum Management: Incentives, Opportunities, and Testing Needed to Enhance Spectrum Sharing*, GAO-13-7 (Washington, D.C.: Nov. 14, 2012).

[45]Presentation to the National Transportation Safety Board. "Positive Train Control: Is it on Track?" FCC, February 27, 2013.

[46]Seven freight railroads (Norfolk Southern, Union Pacific, BNSF, CSX Corporation, Canadian National, Canadian Pacific, and Kansas City Southern) together comprise PTC 220 LLC, a company that owns spectrum licenses. According to a PTC 220 LLC representative, these seven freight railroads will lease spectrum from PTC 220 LLC and will lease spectrum to other railroads based on availability for a fee.

their PTC systems, potentially causing further delays in meeting the 2015 PTC deadline.[47]

By attempting to implement PTC by the 2015 deadline while key components are still in development, railroads may be making choices that could introduce financial and operational risks to PTC implementation. Representatives from freight railroads and FRA officials told us that railroads will not compromise the safety functions of the PTC system and will ensure that systems meet the functionality requirements in RSIA. However, freight railroad representatives told us that in order to work towards testing and installation, they compressed time frames and undertook processes in parallel rather than sequentially. For example, to begin installation while key components were being developed, railroads took a "double touch" approach to equipping locomotives, which involves taking locomotives out of service twice to begin installation while software was being developed.[48] Railroad representatives told us this approach is more expensive than installing the equipment after the software is fully mature, as it involves more labor hours and more time that locomotives are out of service. Our prior work on weapon systems development has shown that technologies that were included in a product development program before they were mature later contributed to cost increases and schedule delays.[49] This work showed that demonstrating a high level of maturity before new technologies are incorporated into a product development plan increases the chances for successful implementation. In 2010, we reported that railroads expected key PTC components to be available by 2012. Railroads have subsequently reported that PTC installation has involved many delays, particularly in component development and many of the essential components are still in development. Consequently, product maturity remains an issue for some PTC components and may result in additional cost and schedule overruns.

---

[47]Amtrak officials also report that securing spectrum has been a major challenge in PTC implementation and has led to implementation delays.

[48]In this case, "double touch" installation refers to partially installing groundwork equipment on thousands of locomotives, which will then later need to be taken out of service again to install the remaining equipment.

[49]GAO-11-133 and GAO, *Joint Strike Fighter: Additional Costs and Delays Risk Not Meeting Warfighter Requirements on Time*, GAO-10-382 (Washington, D.C.: Mar. 19, 2010).

The development time frames involved in implementing PTC by the end of 2015 also potentially introduce operational risks. Representatives from all of the freight railroads we spoke with expressed concern regarding the reliability of PTC and noted that adequate field testing was important to identify and correct problems. These representatives noted that without adequate testing, PTC systems may not perform as planned and may be more prone to system reliability issues, possibly causing service disruptions. FRA officials also expressed concern that if pressured to meet the 2015 deadline, railroads might implement an unreliable PTC system that breaks down and leads to operational inefficiencies through slower trains or congestion.

FRA's Request for Legislative Changes to Provide Additional Authority in Overseeing PTC's Implementation Could Help Manage PTC Implementation

In an August 2012 report to Congress, FRA identified three items for consideration in the event Congress amends RSIA. FRA officials told us that if Congress chooses to amend RSIA, additional authority to extend the deadline on certain rail lines, grant provisional certification of PTC systems and approve the use of alternative safety technologies in lieu of PTC would help them to conduct oversight more effectively by providing FRA flexibility in overseeing PTC. Specifically FRA requested the authority to:

- *Extend the deadline on certain rail lines* to grant railroads incremental deadlines on a case-by-case basis. FRA officials told us they do not want a deadline extension applied to the whole railroad industry. Rather, FRA would like flexibility to create new deadlines based on an individual railroad's circumstances, particularly a railroad's due diligence to achieve the 2015 deadline and efforts to mitigate risks. FRA officials said currently they are unable to approve implementation plans that give completion dates beyond 2015. FRA officials said that such a change would require railroads to update their implementation plans.[50]

- *Grant provisional certification of PTC systems* under controlled conditions before final system completion to allow railroads to operate PTC in certain places while they are still developing it in other places. According to FRA, this would provide assurance that the PTC system was safe, so that a railroad could begin to use the PTC system while

---

[50]Railroads submitted PTC implementation plans in 2010 that, according to FRA, were approved in the same year.

GAO-13-720 Positive Train Control

FRA reviewed the railroad's full safety plan. FRA and railroads told us the benefit of this authority is that it would allow railroads and the public to experience the safety benefits of PTC sooner. FRA officials said they believed this would provide railroads with additional time to address issues and would lead to the implementation of a more reliable system.

- *Approve the use of alternative safety technologies in lieu of PTC* to allow railroads to improve safety and meet many of the functions of PTC through other means. FRA officials told us that they would anticipate using this authority only for commuter and some smaller railroads and would consider technologies in combination with operating rules that railroads demonstrate would enhance safety.

Although some freight railroad representatives we spoke with supported providing FRA with additional authority, others voiced concerns about how the authorities would be administered.[51] For example, details such as how FRA will identify and apply criteria to determine which railroads should receive extensions would need to be addressed. In addition, one freight railroad representative raised concerns over timeliness of FRA's determinations of deadline extensions. Furthermore, representatives from another railroad suggested that granting deadline extensions to some railroads unfairly penalizes those railroads that may meet the PTC deadline. FRA could not provide us with specific information detailing how these authorities would be applied. However, if Congress were to amend RSIA in order to provide FRA additional authorities in implementing PTC, the Secretary of Transportation would need to direct FRA to develop new regulations or orders, in order to carry out its duties.

At a June 2013 hearing on rail safety, AAR and APTA stated their support for FRA's request for additional authority and extending the PTC implementation deadline to December 31, 2018, for all railroads.[52,53] In addition, FRA recommended the Secretary of Transportation be given the

---

[51]We spoke to the four freight railroads included in our study and Amtrak about FRA's requested authorities. However, due to time and resource constraints we did not speak with the seven commuter railroads in our study about these requested authorities.

[52]Edward R. Hamberger, AAR, and Kathryn Waters, APTA, testimony before the Senate Committee on Commerce, Science, and Transportation, June 19, 2013.

[53]Following the June 2013 hearing on rail safety, a Senate bill to extend the deadline for PTC implementation to December 31, 2020, was introduced. S. 1462, 113th Cong. (2013).

authority to grant railroads extensions beyond a December 2018 deadline. In particular, AAR stated its support for FRA's request for flexibility to extend the deadline and previously noted that FRA's request to provide provisional certification of PTC systems could reduce delays. According to AAR, these authorities could provide some relief to railroads experiencing challenges meeting the deadline. APTA, representing commuter railroads, also supported FRA's request for additional authority and specifically stated its support that FRA be allowed to consider alternative technologies in lieu of a PTC system on specified line segments. According to APTA's testimony statement, some commuter railroads already have collision avoidance systems in place that protect against train-to-train collisions. According to APTA, allowing FRA to examine the feasibility of alternative technologies to PTC for some of the smaller railroads on a line-by-line basis could provide opportunities to free up PTC components for other railroads to expedite their PTC implementation.

While an extension of the PTC implementation deadline may provide railroads with additional time to implement PTC, it is not clear that all railroads would be able to meet a revised December 31, 2018 deadline proposed by AAR and APTA. For example, AAR's May 2013 report predicts that, while PTC could be in operation on most mandated PTC routes by December 31, 2018, the date PTC will be in operation on all routes would vary by railroad. One freight railroad we spoke to anticipated it would not be able to fully implement PTC until 2020. In addition, given that many commuter railroads are waiting for freight railroads to develop and implement PTC, many commuter railroads will likely have PTC fully installed after the freight railroads. Furthermore, in a hearing statement, AAR recommended flexibility beyond December 2018 due to the unprecedented nature of PTC and the uncertainties — both known and unknown—of implementation.

Given the uncertainties in implementing PTC and the unexpected delays already encountered, additional challenges could prevent railroads from meeting a new deadline. However, FRA's request for additional authority could provide railroads the flexibility to implement PTC on individual, case-by-case deadlines, either instead of or in addition to an overall deadline extension. Additional authority could also assist FRA in managing its limited staff resources and help railroads mitigate risks and ensure PTC is implemented in a safe and reliable manner. For example, although at the June 2013 rail safety hearing concerns were raised that providing railroads deadline extensions on a case-by-case basis would be resource-intensive and could provide additional challenges and delays, we found that railroads were at various stages in their implementation. Flexibility in extending the deadline for certain railroads acknowledges these differences and also may help FRA better manage limited resources by, for example, preventing a potential review backlog resulting from final safety plans being submitted at the same time—a concern raised by freight railroads and FRA. In addition, according to FRA, allowing provisional certification of PTC systems not only helps to manage limited resources, it also reflects good engineering practice in implementing wide-ranging, complex systems and is a well documented risk mitigation strategy. Finally, as outlined in APTA's testimony at the June 2013 hearing on rail safety, allowing some railroads to use alternative technologies on certain lines could provide relief to other railroads struggling to procure certain PTC components.

FRA Found the Costs of Implementing PTC Outweigh the Safety Benefits, but Opportunities May Exist to Pursue Future Business Benefits

FRA Estimated That the Costs of PTC Implementation Far Outweigh the Safety Benefits

FRA's final regulatory impact analysis for the 2010 final rule estimated that the costs of PTC installation far outweigh the safety benefits.[54] FRA's regulatory impact analysis presents an analysis of the costs and benefits associated with implementing a PTC system on qualifying rail segments. FRA estimated the total costs of implementing PTC to be about $13.2 billion and the total safety benefits to be about $674 million.[55] Costs FRA anticipated to accrue to railroads through the implementation of PTC included:

- development of implementation plans and administrative functions related to the implementation and operation of PTC systems, including the information technology and communication systems that make up the central office;
- hardware costs for onboard locomotive-system components, including installation;
- hardware costs for wayside system components, including installation; and
- maintenance costs for all system components.

FRA expects that PTC implementation will generate safety benefits from the reduction in the risk of certain types of accidents and the number and severity of casualties caused by train accidents on lines equipped with PTC systems. FRA also estimated benefits related to accident preventions that are anticipated to accrue, such as reductions in property damage, equipment cleanup, environmental damage, train delays resulting from track closures, road closures, emergency response, and evacuations. In addition to these safety benefits, FRA's regulatory impact analysis stated that after PTC systems are refined, business benefits

---

[54] FRA also issued a final regulatory impact analysis for the 2012 PTC final rule. The 2012 analysis found that the benefits of the final rule, which were the costs saved by installing PTC on fewer rail lines, outweighed the costs, which represent the increased risk for train incidents as a result of PTC no longer being required along an estimated 10,000 miles of track. The cost saving attributable to the 2012 final rule are not significant enough to affect FRA's conclusion in its previous analysis that the estimated costs of PTC far outweigh the safety benefits.

[55] Dollar amounts are expressed in 2009 dollars and based on a 3-percent discount rate over a 20-year analysis period. OMB guidance recommends that future costs and benefits be discounted using both a 3 percent and 7 percent discount rate. Using a 7 percent discount rate for implementation of PTC, FRA estimated total costs of about $9.55 billion and total benefits of $440 million. Under both discount rates, net benefits are negative, indicating that the rule is not cost beneficial (e.g., economic efficiency would be lower under the rule).

resulting from more efficient railroad operations could be forthcoming. FRA did not, however, include business benefits in its impact analysis estimates because of significant uncertainties regarding whether and when such benefits would be achieved.

FRA Generally Followed OMB Guidance in Assessing the Benefits and Costs of PTC Implementation

We found that FRA generally followed OMB guidance in assessing the benefits and costs of implementing PTC, and although we generally agree with FRA's estimation that costs likely outweigh benefits, we are not confident in the precision of the specific estimates of costs and benefits. Specifically, we compared FRA's regulatory impact analyses with key elements of OMB guidelines, including establishing a baseline, considering alternatives, analyzing uncertainty and quantifying key categories of costs and benefits.[56] We identified some limitations in the analyses, for example, analyses are not comprehensive in some respects and the source and quality of some of the underlying data is unclear. According to FRA officials, the limitations in its analysis and data do not affect the primary outcome of the analysis— that total costs are expected to exceed total safety benefits (i.e., that there are negative net societal benefits). Based on our review, we also believe the limitations we identified were not significant enough to affect FRA's general determination that PTC's implementation costs outweigh benefits. (See app. II for more detail on our assessment of FRA's regulatory impact analyses and findings.)

The PTC mandate limited the flexibility and time available to FRA to develop a rule and analyze its economic impacts; nonetheless, more thorough analyses and better quality data could have made the benefit cost analysis more useful in discussions of PTC implementation. FRA's PTC rulemaking was initiated to implement PTC, as required by RSIA. Specifically, RSIA mandated the installation of a PTC system, which can achieve certain safety benefits, and specified the system's functional requirements and the 2015 implementation deadline. FRA had little latitude to implement other, non-PTC alternatives that may have been less costly to achieve the same safety benefits. In addition, FRA officials told us that because the PTC rulemaking process was expedited, they had to use the information that was available to them at the time to

---

[56]OMB guidelines are intended to inform decision-makers, stakeholders and the public on the benefits and costs of potential regulatory alternatives.

conduct their analysis. However, we found that some information was up to 10 years old and the quality of some of the underlying data was unclear. Finally, FRA excluded business benefits from its estimates, instead opting to include a discussion of potential business benefits in an appendix to its analysis. FRA officials said that they excluded business benefits from their analysis due to uncertainty about whether and when business benefits could be achieved. While we found this decision was appropriate, we found limitations to the discussion of business benefits. For example, FRA assumed that railroads would achieve business benefits associated with a standalone PTC system, but did not include supporting evidence that railroads would likely install such a system.[57]

PTC Alone Is Unlikely to Generate Business Benefits, but Opportunities Might Exist to Pursue Business Benefits over Time and with Additional Investment

Although an overlay PTC system alone is not expected to generate business benefits, over time and with additional investments, there may be opportunities for railroads to achieve some business benefits.[58] PTC implementation involves upgrades that railroads could integrate with existing technologies to provide operational enhancements. As previously discussed, railroads are making substantial investments in their rail network infrastructure to implement PTC. These investments include (1) upgrading existing wayside and office subsystem components; (2) installing a new communication infrastructure to facilitate the communication of train speed, train location, work zone and switch information; (3) and developing detailed geographical information systems (GIS) mappings of an entire rail network. The first two investments can help to generate information that can be shared with other applications, such as train dispatching software and energy management systems to potentially produce business benefits while the detailed GIS mapping can be used to support a railroad's state of good repair.

[57]See FRA Office of Safety Analysis, Positive Train Control Systems Regulatory Impact Analysis, Dec. 8, 2009. In addition, FRA officials told us that the appendix in the 2009 regulatory impact analysis only showed business benefits possible through a PTC standalone system because business benefits are not achievable through an overlay system. In the analysis, FRA stated it believed railroads would add a productivity system to PTC that would enable them to achieve these benefits.

[58]As previously mentioned, most railroads are implementing an overlay PTC system. However, additional investment in a standalone PTC system may also provide opportunities for railroads to achieve business benefits by allowing for the elimination of signal systems found in the overlay system.

More specific train location and speed data for use in other applications such as precision dispatching could help to improve train dispatching, potentially increasing network capacity.[59] The PTC overlay systems railroads are installing require changes to most dispatching systems to account for more precise train location information. For example, according to AAR and FRA, most railroad dispatching systems, which currently require location information within one-tenth of a mile, are being upgraded as part of PTC to require location information of up to a ten-thousandth of a mile. According to a freight railroad representative we spoke to, using the more detailed train location information from PTC could help dispatchers better prioritize train movements based on a train's delivery schedule and better manage "meet and pass" operations (when two trains approach each other on a single track). PTC, however, is not a prerequisite for precision dispatching. For example, one freight railroad representative told us that their railroad is already using alternative means independent of PTC to enable real-time train position reporting to improve dispatching. Nonetheless, the PTC system that is being installed is also expected to provide this information. In addition, according to a supplier we included in our review, PTC could enable development of additional features, such as precision dispatching. Representatives from another supplier we spoke with said they anticipate that railroads will use PTC-generated train location information for improved dispatching in the future after the initial rollout of PTC.

PTC-generated information and data also could help railroads achieve greater fuel savings than they are currently achieving with their energy management systems. An energy management system is an on-board technology that uses a variety of information, including train location and track elevation and curvature, to calculate a train's most fuel efficient run and make throttle and braking recommendations to the operator to minimize a train's consumption of fuel.[60,61] PTC can generate information

[59]Precision or optimized dispatching is the use of complex computer algorithms to analyze and account for a number of conditions to determine optimal scheduling that can lead to increased capacity, reduced transit times, and fuel savings resulting from reduced train idle times.

[60]Fuel efficient runs optimize train mechanics by using less braking when possible and utilizing a train's potential energy to coast to reduce the amount of fuel a train uses while traveling from origin to destination. Energy management systems determine the most fuel efficient run by running a number of simulations of a train's potential route then picking the best scenario that conserves the most energy and fuel.

that could assist energy management systems in two ways. First, PTC systems are being designed to enforce compliance with safety parameters, such as speed restrictions, that trains encounter when traveling from origin to destination. According to an energy management system supplier and freight railroad representatives we spoke with, these parameters could be used to make train movement calculations based on the PTC safety parameters governing the route, which is information currently unavailable to such systems.[62] Second, railroads are developing more detailed mapping of their rail networks, including its critical features such as signals and switches and putting this information into a track database as part of PTC implementation. According to an energy management system supplier we spoke with, this more precise information, which is needed for the PTC system to calculate train safety stopping distances could enhance railroads' existing fuel-management systems' performance through more accurate information on track features.

Representatives from all of the freight railroads we spoke with reported already achieving fuel savings through energy management systems but noted that there may be potential for additional savings by integrating these systems with these PTC components. For example, one freight railroad representative reported that the railroad's energy management system currently provides annual fuel savings of 4 to 6 percent, but that integrating the system with PTC could lead to an additional 1 to 2 percent in fuel savings.

Freight railroad officials we spoke with generally expressed interest in pursuing PTC-related business benefits, but noted they are currently focused on installing PTC and are devoting their time and resources to that effort.[63] For example, one freight railroad representative told us the railroad has not had time to fully think through how to achieve business benefits using the PTC system since all resources are currently focused on implementing PTC and noted that these benefits were incremental and

[61]Freight railroads are currently using two energy management systems. LEADER is manufactured by New York Air Brake, and Trip Optimizer is manufactured by General Electric.

[62]According to one freight railroad, energy management systems currently take speed restrictions into account.

[63]By contrast, only one of the seven commuter railroads we spoke to expressed interest in pursuing business benefits through PTC. Several commuter railroad representatives told us their systems are already designed to allow optimal rush hour capacity.

could likely be achieved outside of PTC. However, railroad representatives from the four freight railroads we spoke with said they would explore ways to leverage the safety investment they are making in PTC to obtain additional business benefits once the PTC system is fully implemented and operating. These railroads emphasized that pursuing business benefits will involve additional investments beyond their current investments in PTC installation.

Nevertheless, railroad representatives also identified a number of concerns about attempting to achieve business benefits through PTC systems. First, some business benefits are already being achieved through existing technologies. Second, the potential for significant PTC business benefits is still not clear. For example, according to one railroad representative, despite his railroad's long history with PTC, it is still unsure of the potential for PTC to achieve business benefits. PTC is a new technology, and system components are still being developed. After the safety functionalities of the system have been tested and deployed, representatives will be able to determine what additional functionality (e.g., operational efficiencies) can be achieved through PTC implementation. In addition, additional functionalities to achieve PTC business benefits must be done in a way that would not compromise the system's underlying safety functions. FRA officials told us that when integrating PTC with other systems to achieve business benefits, railroads must be careful not to compromise the integrity of PTC system's underlying safety functions. According to a PTC supplier, delaying the introduction of any business benefit features to the PTC system may help railroads avoid complicating the initial deployment of PTC. Representatives from one freight railroad we spoke with anticipated that railroads would, with additional investment, begin to achieve business benefits through PTC over the next two decades as PTC is fully installed and operational.

Conclusions

In the wake of the 2008 Chatsworth commuter rail accident that resulted in 25 deaths and over 100 injuries, RSIA was enacted, marking a public policy decision that rail safety warranted mandatory and accelerated PTC system installation. PTC implementation is a massive, complex, and expensive undertaking. Amid numerous implementation challenges, it appears that most railroads will not fully implement PTC by the December 31, 2015, deadline. Given the state of PTC technology and the myriad of PTC components that must seamlessly work together, the potential risks railroads may be taking in attempting to meet the deadline should be considered. Accordingly, FRA has requested additional authorities which could allow FRA to better manage its limited resources and give railroads the flexibility to take a more measured approach to PTC implementation, potentially mitigating some implementation risks. AAR and others have proposed extending the PTC implementation deadline to December 31, 2018, and agree that providing FRA with additional authorities could increase flexibility in managing PTC implementation. Given all the uncertainties in implementing PTC technology, it is not clear 2018 will be sufficient time for railroads to fully implement PTC. Consequently, Congress, the railroads, and FRA may end up in the same position they are currently in, with an impending deadline and not enough flexibility to ensure that all railroads fully implement PTC both reliably and expediently. Regardless of whether the deadline is extended for the industry as a whole or FRA is given the flexibility to grant extensions to railroads on a case-by-case basis—upon consideration of railroads' due diligence in implementing PTC—action is needed to help FRA better manage its limited resources and address the reality of PTC implementation, which is that different railroads are at different stages.

Matters for Congressional Consideration

To help ensure that the Federal Railroad Administration manages its limited resources and provides flexibility to railroads in implementing PTC, Congress should consider amending RSIA as requested in the FRA's August 2012 PTC Implementation Status Report to Congress, including granting FRA the authority to:

- extend the deadline on individual rail lines—when the need to do so can be demonstrated by the railroad and verified by FRA—to grant railroads incremental deadlines based on a case-by-case basis;
- grant provisional certification of PTC systems under controlled conditions before final system completion; and
- approve the use of alternative safety technologies in lieu of PTC to allow railroads to improve safety and meet many of the functions of PTC through other means.

Agency Comments

We provided a draft of this report to the Secretary of Transportation for review and comment. DOT provided technical comments, which we incorporated as appropriate.

As agreed with your office, unless you publicly announce the contents of this report earlier, we plan no further distribution until 30 days from the report date. At that time, we will send copies to the Secretary of

Transportation and other interested parties. In addition, the report will be available at no charge on the GAO website at http://www.gao.gov.

If you or your staff have any questions about this report, please contact me at (202) 512-4431 or flemingS@gao.gov. Contact points for our Offices of Congressional Relations and Public Affairs may be found on the last page of this report. GAO staff who made major contributions to this report are listed in appendix III.

Sincerely yours,

Susan A. Fleming
Director, Physical Infrastructure Issues

Appendix I: Objectives, Scope, and Methodology

This report discusses (1) how railroads are implementing positive train control (PTC) and the challenges, if any, to meeting the PTC implementation deadline; and (2) FRA's estimates of the benefits and costs of PTC and the extent to which railroads might be able to leverage PTC technology to achieve business benefits.

To obtain information about how railroads are implementing PTC and the challenges to meeting the PTC implementation deadline, we interviewed representatives from the four largest Class I freight railroads—BNSF Railway, CSX Corporation, Norfolk Southern, and Union Pacific—and Amtrak. We also interviewed representatives from seven commuter railroads:[1]

- Massachusetts Bay Transportation Authority (Boston, Massachusetts)
- Metropolitan Transportation Authority (MTA) Long Island Railroad (New York, New York)
- MTA Metro-North Railroad (New York, New York)
- Southern California Regional Rail Authority, also known as Metrolink (Los Angeles, California)
- Southeastern Pennsylvania Transportation Authority (SEPTA) (Philadelphia, Pennsylvania),
- Utah Transit Authority (Salt Lake City, Utah)
- Virginia Railway Express (Washington, D.C.)

We selected the commuter railroads to represent a range of geographic locations, levels of ridership, and PTC implementation status, while selecting railroads that had a mix of operations, including those operating on tracks owned by all four of the largest Class I railroads and Amtrak. We also interviewed or received written responses from representatives from selected rail supply companies (New York Air Brake, Wabtec, MeteorComm, and Parsons); railroad industry associations (the Association of American Railroads (AAR), the American Short Line and Regional Railroad Association, and American Public Transportation Association (APTA)); the Chlorine Institute; six experts; and FRA. We selected the railroad supply companies based on the types of products and services provided, railroad clients, and recommendations from FRA, associations, and experts. We selected experts based on their experience

---

[1]We spoke to the four freight railroads included in our study and Amtrak about FRA's requested authorities. However, due to time and resource constraints we did not speak with the seven commuter railroads in our study about these requested authorities.

working on PTC, independence from current PTC work, and
recommendations from associations and other experts. We also reviewed
PTC development and implementation requirements in the Rail Safety
Improvement Act of 2008 and FRA regulations; FRA's 2012 report to
Congress on Positive Train Control Implementation Status, Issues, and
Impacts; and prior GAO reports. We attended the Railway Age
International Conference on Communications-Based Train Control in
Washington, D.C., and the National Transportation Safety Board Forum
on Positive Train Control Implementation. We visited and met with
officials at Southern California Regional Rail Authority, in Los Angeles,
California, and Amtrak officials in Wilmington, Delaware, to witness
computer simulations of PTC and view PTC track side components. In
addition, we visited and met with officials at SEPTA in Philadelphia,
Pennsylvania.

To understand how FRA estimated the benefits and costs of PTC in its
rulemakings we reviewed the 2010 and 2012 PTC rules and the
supporting proposed and final regulatory impact analyses, and
interviewed representatives from the FRA. To review the quality of the
regulatory impact analyses, we used key elements in the OMB economic
guidelines (*Circular A-4*) as criteria, including: use of appropriate baseline
from which to estimate benefits and costs; assessment of a range of
alternatives; inclusion of all key categories of benefits and costs; use of
best available information in analyzing benefits and costs; and analysis of
uncertainty. In addition, to better understand the potential economic effect
of the rules, and the changes that FRA made in response to comments,
we reviewed public comments submitted to FRA in response to the
rulemakings, and we interviewed FRA officials, stakeholder groups (AAR,
the Chlorine Institute), PTC technology and railroad industry experts,
economists, and railway supply companies. We did not independently
analyze the benefits and costs of FRA's PTC regulations. Since the
rulemaking is in response to a mandate, we focused on the information
contained in the benefit cost analyses and did not comment on the overall
rule.

To determine the extent to which railroads might be able to leverage PTC
technology to achieve business benefits we interviewed representatives
from the previously mentioned Class I freight railroads, Amtrak, 7
commuter railroads, association officials, experts, railroad supply
companies, and FRA to learn about plans to leverage PTC to achieve
business benefits as well as existing technologies that could potentially
be used to achieve business benefits. We reviewed documentation from
an array of sources, including FRA, AAR, the Chlorine Institute, and PTC

experts to determine the types of technology that could potentially be used to achieve PTC business benefits and the extent railroads can leverage PTC technology to achieve business benefits.

Appendix II: Observations on the Quality of FRA's Regulatory Impact Analyses Used in PTC Rulemaking

FRA issued regulatory impact analyses that examined the economic impact of the implementation of RSIA and generally found that the costs far outweighed the benefits of PTC installation.[1] Specifically, the December 2009 final regulatory impact analysis concluded that the costs to comply with the regulation far exceeded the safety benefits of PTC. The January 2012 final regulatory impact analysis evaluated the costs and benefits of the final rule (i.e., to eliminate the two risk-based tests for exempting certain rail segments from the PTC requirement) and found that the benefits, which were the costs saved by installing PTC on fewer rail lines, outweigh the costs, which were the increased risk for train incidents as a result of PTC no longer being required along 10,000 miles of track. However, this final rule did not alter the conclusions of the December 2009 analysis conclusion that the costs of PTC far outweighed the safety benefits.

We reviewed FRA's 2009 and 2012 regulatory impact analyses using OMB guidance for developing regulatory impact analyses and found that although FRA generally followed OMB guidance in assessing the costs and benefits of implementing PTC, the quality of some of the underlying data suggests some limitations in the analyses. Specifically, we found:

- Although FRA established a baseline and considered one alternative, an analysis of other alternatives in the implementation of PTC may have been useful.

- FRA analyzed uncertainty associated with cost estimates, but not with safety benefit estimates.

- FRA included key costs in its analysis, but excluded the cost of implementation to the government.

- Data and computations underlying the analysis were not clearly sourced and explained, and for some data, the quality was unclear resulting in a lack of transparency.

See Table 2 for a discussion of these findings, including the OMB guidance, what FRA did in the December 2009 analysis, what FRA did in the January 2012 analysis, and our analysis.

---

[1]FRA determined that the 2010 PTC rule and 2012 PTC final rule were significant and as directed by Executive Order 12866, analyzed the regulatory impacts.

Appendix II: Observations on the Quality of
FRA's Regulatory Impact Analyses Used in
PTC Rulemaking

Table 2: Comparison of the Federal Railroad Administration's Positive Train Control Economic Analysis to OMB's guidelines

OMB Guideline	What FRA did in 2009 analysis	What FRA did in 2012 analysis	GAO's analysis
FRA considered one alternative against a baseline, though analysis of other alternatives could have been useful			
Measure the potential benefits and costs of regulatory alternatives incremental to a "baseline" (or the conditions that would exist in the absence of the proposed regulation).	Used a baseline that reflected the policy conditions of the time of RSIA to estimate the effects of the PTC rule. Analyzed one alternative that used: - traffic levels from base year 2008. FRA officials said this was the best approach because it used actual 2008 traffic data rather than projected 2015 data for railroads' implementation plans. - the RSIA-mandated December 31, 2015 implementation deadline.	Used the 2010 rule as the baseline. Used projected traffic levels from 2015, which reduced the PTC implementation cost and the safety benefit estimates.	FRA established a baseline as required but could have analyzed other alternatives in the first analysis to better inform decision making, such as: - analyze other years for base years of traffic. For example, if FRA had used an estimate of 2015 traffic levels in the 2009 analysis, it would have likely shown lower costs. Railroads, for example, could reduce PTC compliance costs by consolidating some traffic by the 2015 deadline. FRA indicated it did not receive the railroads' projections of 2015 traffic levels until 2011, after FRA completed its 2009 analysis. However, FRA could have developed an estimate of expected traffic in 2015 to assess how benefits and costs would vary under alternative base-year traffic levels. - longer implementation time frames, which could have shown lower costs. FRA discussed the potential for a longer time period to lower costs. FRA officials noted and we agree that FRA was under time constraints and that a longer implementation deadline was not feasible since PTC was mandated. However, the mandate did not prohibit FRA from analyzing alternatives.
FRA quantified safety benefits and most key categories of costs			
Assess the social benefits and costs of each alternative, including those that can be quantified and providing a qualitative discussion of benefits and costs that cannot be quantified.	Quantified safety benefits and most key categories of costs, specifically the safety benefits and compliance costs associated with PTC installation. Did not include government administrative costs, which OMB directs agencies to include if they are significant. Excluded business benefits from its primary analysis and instead presented estimates of business benefits in an appendix. FRA presented the benefits of a standalone PTC system and stated it believed railroads would add a productivity system to PTC	Quantified benefits (cost savings associated with not having to install PTC on certain segments), and costs (damages associated with increased risk of accidents). FRA did not analyze the effect of the final rule on business benefits. The agency acknowledged that there are limitations in the analysis underlying the business benefit estimates in the 2009 regulatory impact analysis, stating	Estimates of government costs would have been useful. However, FRA officials said they didn't include government administrative costs because they viewed the activities as part of their safety mandate, they do not typically include these costs in such analyses, the costs were relatively small, and they did not think including these costs would have affected PTC decision making. We believe the inclusion of these costs could have better informed decision making. Although it was reasonable for FRA to consider whether the 2010 PTC regulation might generate business benefits, FRA's business benefits estimates are of questionable usefulness and reliability.

Appendix II: Observations on the Quality of
FRA's Regulatory Impact Analyses Used in
PTC Rulemaking

OMB Guideline	What FRA did in 2009 analysis	What FRA did in 2012 analysis	GAO's analysis
	that would enable them to achieve these benefits. According to FRA, it included these benefits because at the time there was a possibility that railroads would adopt a PTC system capable of generating business benefits.	that many of these benefits were speculative or achievable through other means, and that existing PTC systems lack some of the features used to justify assumptions in the 2004 report's analysis. FRA stated that it had no reason to believe that railroads were investing in PTC-related equipment likely to generate business benefits. According to FRA, the railroads' PTC implementation plans submitted to FRA after the 2010 rule had no plans for implementing PTC systems that would generate business benefits in the 20-year analysis period.	FRA based its analysis on a 2004 study that FRA acknowledged used controversial assumptions to determine whether PTC would generate business benefits. This report was of questionable validity (see below) but FRA noted it did not have time to formally update the study. Furthermore, the agency did not consider business benefits in its 2012 final rule, stating that many of these benefits were achievable through other means and that FRA had no reason to believe that railroads would achieve business benefits through PTC.

The 2009 discussion also presented the benefits of a standalone system but did not provide evidence that railroads would install such a system. The analysis could have been enhanced if it had taken into account the potential business benefits of an overlay system. |
| **FRA analyzed uncertainty associated with costs but not safety benefits** | | | |
| Uncertainty should be analyzed and presented in terms of both a central "best estimate," which reflects the expected value of the benefits and costs of the rule, as well as a description of the ranges of plausible values for benefits, costs, and net benefits, which informs decision-makers and the public of the degree of uncertainty associated with the regulatory decision. | Analyzed the uncertainty associated with each of the three main categories of cost (central office, locomotive, and wayside), and discount rate.

Did not analyze the uncertainty associated with PTC safety benefits. FRA did not analyze the uncertainty associated with benefits because, according to officials, the gap between the expected costs and benefits was significant enough that uncertainty in the benefits could not have affected the results. | Analyzed uncertainty associated with miles of rail segments receiving exemption, and discount rate. | FRA's approach to analyzing the uncertainty of costs was generally consistent with OMB guidance (only partially addressed). FRA also generally followed OMB guidelines in discounting future benefits and costs using OMB-recommended discount rates.

A discussion of uncertainties of PTC safety benefits could have been useful. For example, PTC might work better or worse than expected in terms of accident prevention. Such a discussion may have been useful given that there is no existing fully functional PTC system for safety purposes to use to analyze its effectiveness in preventing accidents and that agency judgment was the primary source of safety information. |

Appendix II: Observations on the Quality of
FRA's Regulatory Impact Analyses Used in
PTC Rulemaking

OMB Guideline	What FRA did in 2009 analysis	What FRA did in 2012 analysis	GAO's analysis
Quality of some FRA data sources is unclear			
Regulatory analysis should be transparent and the results must be reproducible. A regulatory analysis should document that results are based on the best reasonably obtainable scientific, technical, and economic information available.[a]	Relied mostly on a 1999 Railroad Safety Advisory Committee (RSAC) report for cost and benefits information Business benefits discussion relied on a 2004 report that FRA and others have called into question and that FRA acknowledged was controversial.	Relied on same 1999 report for cost and benefit information. FRA acknowledged limitations in the business benefits estimates it included in the 2009 regulatory analysis.	FRA's analysis provides little information about the origin of its data sources. We could not reproduce certain computations in order to determine reasonableness of the estimates, as OMB guidelines recommend. This raises questions regarding the quality of the data, particularly since FRA's analysis was based on data from a 1999 report that was approximately 10 years old at the time FRA used its estimates.[b] FRA officials noted that they did not receive objections to their estimates in the public comment phase of the 2010 rulemaking.[c] However, it is not clear whether there was enough information in the rulemaking to be able to comment on the quality of the data. FRA said it relied on the 2004 analysis for its 2009 business benefits appendix because it was the only information available at the time.

Source: GAO.

[a]OMB guidelines also direct agencies to comply with their own information quality guidelines. The Department of Transportation issued guidelines in 2002

[b]The 1999 report defined PTC as a system designed to prevent train-to-train collisions, enforce speed restrictions, and provide protection for roadway workers. FRA's 2010 PTC rule includes an additional requirement, to prevent movement through a switch in the wrong position.

[c]Because the 2012 rulemaking relied on essentially the same data, the same data limitations apply.

Appendix III: GAO Contact and Staff Acknowledgments

GAO Contact	Susan A. Fleming, (202) 512-2834 or Flemings@gao.gov
Staff Acknowledgments	In addition to the contact named above, Sharon Silas, Assistant Director; Richard Bulman; Tim Guinane; Delwen Jones; Emily Larson; Sara Ann Moessbauer; Josh Ormond; Madhav Panwar and Crystal Wesco made key contributions to this report.